MW01014055

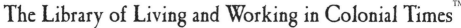

A Day in the Life of a Colonial Miller

Laurie Krebs

The Rosen Publishing Group's
PowerKids Press™
New York

For my friends at the Keeler Tavern Museum

Published in 2004 by The Rosen Publishing Group, Inc.
29 East 21st Street, New York, NY 10010

First Edition

Editor: Frances E. Ruffin
Book Design: Emily Muschinske

Photo Credits: Cover and title page, pp. 4, 7, 8, 11, 15, 16, 19 © North Wind Picture Archives. p. 12 © Underwood & Underwood/CORBIS; p. 20 © Hulton/Archive/Getty Images.

Krebs, Laurie.
A day in the life of a colonial miller / Laurie Krebs.— 1st ed.
    p. cm. — (The library of living and working in colonial times)
Summary: Describes a day in the life of a Connecticut miller during the Revolutionary War, how his gristmill operated, how he kept his tools clean, and what happened when British troops approached. Includes bibliographical references (p.   ) and index.
  ISBN 0-8239-6230-X (lib bdg.)
1. Keeler, Isaac, ca. 1715–1778—Juvenile literature. 2. Millers—Connecticut—Ridgefield—History—18th century—Juvenile literature. [1. Keeler, Isaac, ca. 1715–1778. 2. Millers. 3. Water mills. 4. Connecticut—History—Colonial period, ca. 1600–1775. 5. United States—History—Colonial period, ca. 1600–1775.] I. Title. II. Series.
  HD8039.M562 U55 2003
  664'.72'092—dc21

                                                                        2002000099

Manufactured in the United States of America

Isaac Keeler and his gristmill actually existed. He was a miller who lived and worked in Ridgefield, Connecticut. The Battle of Ridgefield actually occurred on April 27, 1777. Descriptions of Mr. Keeler's day-to-day responsibilities were fictionalized, but the details of colonial milling and colonial life are true.

Contents

Isaac Keeler, Miller

April 27, 1777, was like most spring mornings in colonial New England. Having risen at dawn, Isaac Keeler of Ridgefield, Connecticut, made his way to his **gristmill** to begin the day. In the room where customers would wait, Isaac swept the floor and blew dust from a checkerboard. He took down stools from pegs on the wall. In the main room, he brushed away yesterday's milling dust of fine grains of corn. Milling dust could catch fire. Fires were common in gristmills. Isaac kept his mill as clean as possible.

◀ *A miller was one of the most important men in a colonial town.*

The Mill Covenant

Early colonists ground their grain by hand to make flour for their bread. This was hard work. When new towns were formed, a miller was invited to live there. He was given a choice piece of land near a stream or river where he could build a mill.

In 1716, Ridgefield's first miller signed a paper promising to grind the villagers' grain two days each week. He could keep a small amount of **meal** as a payment. This promise was called a Mill **Covenant**. Future millers, such as Isaac, signed this paper, too.

This is a woodcut of an old mill that was built in New England. ▶

The Power of Water

To get enough water to power his mill, Isaac built a dam that held back water and formed a pond. A waterwheel, with wooden boards or buckets that resemble Ferris wheel seats, sat at the edge of his millpond. Isaac opened a gate in the dam, and water rushed from a narrow channel into the top bucket of the wheel. As that bucket filled, it moved down and around like the hands on a clock. This allowed the next bucket to fill. The second bucket moved down, then a third, until the wheel turned in a steady **rhythm**.

◀ *Gristmills were operated by waterpower from rivers or streams.*

Gearing Up for Business

A heavy oak beam called a shaft was connected to the waterwheel. It ran under the mill to a set of gears that changed the power's direction. As the waterwheel and the shaft turned, their gears turned an upright pole called a **spindle**. The power from the spindle passed through two **millstones** on the floor above. It turned the top stone, which was the grinding stone. Isaac entered the **loft**, where several bags of grain awaited his attention. His friend John Barlow would soon arrive to pick up his cornmeal.

The waterwheel was connected to a huge oak beam called a shaft. ▶

In the Hopper

Isaac poured the corn into the grain bin and watched it collect in the hopper below. The hopper was an open bin that funneled grain into the center of the millstones.

To judge the quality of John Barlow's grain, Isaac used his "miller's thumb," rolling a bit of grain between his thumb and finger. Depending on the age of the corn and how moist it was, Isaac would **adjust** the speed of the wheel to determine how finely the stones cut the corn. He poured oil on some scraps of wool and began to oil the mill's machinery.

◀ *This modern-day miller is shown funneling corn down a hopper.*

The Daily Grind

Two disk-shaped grinding stones were laid at the heart of Isaac's gristmill. The bottom disk was set in the floor and never moved. The upper disk was turned by spindle power. Each stone was cut with a pattern of **furrows** which were narrow near the center and wider at the edges. The cut sides of the stones faced each other. As the grain fell between them, it was ground into smooth meal. The furrows guided the meal to the outer edge of the stones. It fell into a bin called a meal **trough**. Isaac then scooped the meal into sacks.

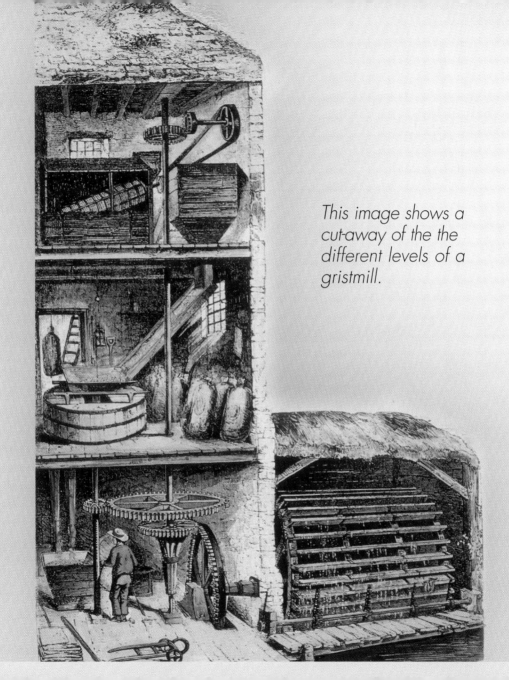

This image shows a cut-away of the the different levels of a gristmill.

Dressing the Stones

Isaac knew that dull millstones spoiled the quality of good grain. The meal became gummy and rotted quickly. Isaac saw that his millstones were sharp and properly "dressed."

In spring he separated the stones to recut the furrows with a hammerlike tool called a **chisel**. Then he attached a thin, sharp stick to the spindle. If a full circle was scratched on the bottom stone, Isaac knew that the spindle was turning evenly. The stones felt sharp. The scratching was clear. The dressing was complete.

◄ *A miller had to make sure that the furrows on his stones were sharp.*

Isaac Keeler, Patriot

The American colonies had been at war with Britain for nearly a year. As did other **patriots**, Isaac wanted to be free from British rule. He collected supplies for the **militia** and kept them in his gristmill.

On that spring day, Isaac's friend John Barlow rushed into the mill. Out of breath, he told Isaac that the British had set fire to patriot storehouses in nearby Danbury, Connecticut. The troops were planning to return to the **sound** by a route that would take them through Ridgefield, right past Isaac's mill.

Many colonial men served in local militias to fight the British. ▶

The British Are Coming

John Barlow's corn lay forgotten in the meal trough as Isaac hurried outside to close the gate to the millpond. The noisy rhythm of the waterwheel creaked to a stop.

He ran to tell his wife, Hannah, and sent her to a cousin's home in town where she would be safe. Then he raced to the field where his sons, Elijah and Josiah, were planting spring crops. They grabbed their **muskets** and headed for the village to join the militia. In the distance, Isaac heard the beat of drums. The British were coming!

◄ *The fight for freedom took place in many colonies. These colonial soldiers faced the British in Lexington, Massachusetts.*

The Battle of Ridgefield

Come they did, setting fire to the homes of patriots, killing cattle, and stealing food. The villagers built a wall of logs and stones across the road to block British troops. The militia fought bravely. It had few weapons and little training. The battle did not last long. In the end, the British marched into town and camped in a nearby churchyard. Isaac Keeler was not surprised to find his gristmill burned, but he might have been surprised to know that 225 years later, he is remembered as an honest miller and a brave patriot.

Glossary

adjust (uh-JUST) To change.

chisel (CHIH-zel) A tool with a strong blade and a sharp edge for chipping wood or stone.

covenant (KUHV-nuhnt) A written agreement or promise.

furrows (FUR-ohz) Long, narrow grooves or tracks.

gristmill (GRIST-mil) A mill that grinds grain.

loft (LAHFT) An upper room or floor in a building.

meal (MEEL) Grain that has been ground.

militia (muh-LIH-shuh) A group of people who are trained and ready to fight in an emergency.

millstones (MIL-stohnz) Circular stones used for grinding grain.

muskets (MUS-kits) Guns with long barrels used in battle and hunting.

patriots (PAY-tree-uhts) People who love and defend their country.

rhythm (RIH-thum) An orderly pattern of movement.

sound (SOWND) A long, narrow body of water that lies between a mainland and an island.

spindle (SPIN-duhl) A rod or pin used to turn a machine part.

trough (TRAHF) A long, narrow container for food or drink.

Index

Primary Sources

Cover, pages 4, 11, 16. *Details and illustrations from a woodcut of an old mill, built on the island of Nantucket, Massachusetts (1879). Illustrator: Wendell Mary (1879). From Harper's Weekly.* **Page 8.** *View of Carve's Mill at Sleepy Hollow, Tarrytown, New York. Illustrator, W.R. Miller (1853). From Gleason's Pictorial.* **Page 19.** *A whetstone mill. Illustrator unknown (1879). From American Agriculturalist,* **Page 20.** *Minutemen facing British soldiers on Lexington Common, Massachusetts, in the first battle in the War of Independence; April 19, 1775. British artist, William Barnes Wollen (1857–1936). Hulton Archives.*

Web Sites

Due to the changing nature of Internet links, PowerKids Press has developed an online list of Web sites related to the subject of this book. The site is updated regularly. Please use this link to access the list:
www.powerkidslinks.com/llwct/dlcmill/